Borders & Motifs
IN CROSS STITCH

■

Gail Bussi

MEREHURST

THE CHARTS

Some of the designs in this book are very detailed and due to inevitable space limitations, the charts may be shown on a comparatively small scale; in such cases, readers may find it helpful to have the particular chart with which they are currently working enlarged.

THREADS

The projects in this book were all stitched with DMC stranded cotton embroidery threads. The keys given with each chart also list thread combinations for those who wish to use Anchor or Madeira threads. It should be pointed out that the shades produced by different companies vary slightly, and it is not always possible to find identical colours in a different range.

Published in 1994 by Merehurst Limited
Ferry House, 51-57 Lacy Road, Putney, London SW15 1PR
Text © Copyright 1994
Photography & illustrations © Copyright 1994 Merehurst Limited
ISBN 1 85391 382 0

A catalogue record for this book is available from the British Library.

Managing Editor Heather Dewhurst
Edited by Diana Lodge
Designed by Maggie Aldred
Photography by Marie-Louise Avery
Illustrations by John Hutchinson
Typesetting by Dacorum Type & Print, Hemel Hempstead
Colour separation by Fotographics Limited, UK – Hong Kong
Printed in Italy by G Canale & C SpA

Merehurst is the leading publisher of craft books and has an excellent range of titles to suit all levels. Please send to the address above for our free catalogue, stating the title of this book.

CONTENTS

INTRODUCTION

Counted cross stitch is undoubtedly one of the most versatile and creative forms of needlework, which accounts for its tremendous increase in popularity over the last few years. Its appeal also rests in the fact that, with just a few simple stitches and techniques, even an inexperienced needleworker has the tools to create a vast range of delightful designs.

Borders and individual motifs in cross stitch are among the most traditional design elements of this type of needlework, as can be seen from a study of the samplers of past centuries, with their charming stylized motifs and repeating borders.

In this book I have tried to give a wide range of different styles and types of borders and motifs, allowing for varied interests and levels of ability. The designs presented here are suitable for celebrating and commemorating special occasions, for decorating items for the home, or for making very special gifts. They will, hopefully, serve as a springboard for your own imagination. This is intended as a source book of ideas and inspiration for all

BASIC SKILLS

BEFORE YOU BEGIN

PREPARING THE FABRIC
Even with an average amount of handling, many evenweave fabrics tend to fray at the edges, so it is a good idea to overcast the raw edges, using ordinary sewing thread, before you begin.

FABRIC
Many of the projects in this book use Aida fabric, which is ideal both for beginners and more advanced stitchers as it has a surface of clearly designated squares. All Aida fabric has a count, which refers to the number of squares (each stitch covers one square) to one inch (2.5cm); the higher the count, the smaller the finished stitching. Other projects in this book use either damask Aida, described below, or Hardanger – a pure cotton evenweave. This is woven with a double thread, which counts as one.

Damask Aida, a luxury look Aida fabric, has been used for one of the projects in 'A Floral Alphabet'. Available in both 14- and 18-count versions, this Aida fabric has a slightly glossy finish and is increasingly popular, particularly for designs intended for special occasions or to be used for gifts.

THE INSTRUCTIONS
Each project begins with a full list of the materials that you will require. The measurements given for the embroidery fabric include a minimum of 5cm (2in) all around to allow for stretching it in a frame and preparing the edges to prevent them from fraying.

Colour keys for stranded embroidery cottons – DMC, Anchor or Madeira – are given with each chart. It is assumed that you will need to buy one skein of each colour mentioned in a particular key, even though you may use less, but where two or more skeins are needed, this information is included in the main list of requirements.

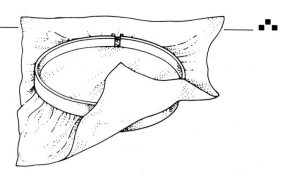

To work from the charts, particularly those where several symbols are used in close proximity, some readers may find it helpful to have the chart enlarged so that the squares and symbols can be seen more easily. Many photocopying services will do this for a minimum charge.

Before you begin to embroider, always mark the centre of the design with two lines of basting stitches, one vertical and one horizontal, running from edge to edge of the fabric, as indicated by the arrows on the charts.

As you stitch, use the centre lines given on the chart and the basting threads on your fabric as reference points for counting the squares and threads to position your design accurately.

WORKING IN A HOOP

A hoop is the most popular frame for use with small areas of embroidery. It consists of two rings, one fitted inside the other; the outer ring usually has an adjustable screw attachment so that it can be tightened to hold the stretched fabric in place. Hoops are available in several sizes, ranging from 10cm (4in) in diameter to quilting hoops with a diameter of 38cm (15in). Hoops with table stands or floor stands attached are also available.

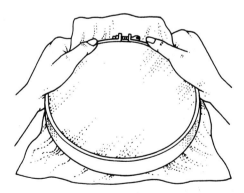

1 To stretch your fabric in a hoop, place the area to be embroidered over the inner ring and press the outer ring over it, with the tension screw released. Tissue paper can be placed between the outer ring and the embroidery, so that the hoop does not mark the fabric. Lay the tissue paper over the fabric when you set it in the hoop, then tear away the central embroidery area.

2 Smooth the fabric and, if necessary, straighten the grain before tightening the screw. The fabric should be evenly stretched.

WORKING IN A RECTANGULAR FRAME

Rectangular frames are more suitable for larger pieces of embroidery. They consist of two rollers, with tapes attached, and two side pieces, which slot into the rollers and are held in place by pegs or screw attachments. Available in different sizes, either alone or with adjustable table or floor stands, frames are measured by the length of the roller tape, and range in size from 30cm (12in) to 68cm (27in).

As alternatives to a slate frame, canvas stretchers and the backs of old picture frames can be used. Provided there is sufficient extra fabric around the finished size of the embroidery, the edges can be turned under and simply attached with drawing pins (thumb tacks) or staples.

1 To stretch your fabric in a rectangular frame, cut out the fabric, allowing at least an extra 5cm (2in) all around the finished size of the embroidery. Baste a single 12mm (½in) turning on the top and bottom edges and oversew strong tape, 2.5cm (1in) wide, to the other two sides. Mark the centre line both ways with basting stitches. Working from the centre outward and using strong thread, oversew the top and bottom edges to the roller tapes. Fit the side pieces into the slots, and roll any extra fabric on one roller.

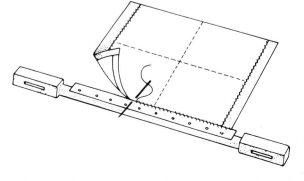

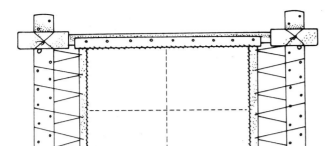

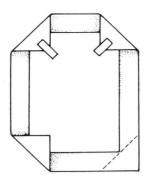

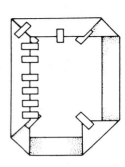

2 Insert the pegs or adjust the screw attachments to secure the frame. Thread a large-eyed needle (chenille needle) with strong thread or fine string and lace both edges, securing the ends around the intersections of the frame. Lace the webbing at 2.5cm (1in) intervals, stretching the fabric evenly.

1 Place embroidery face down, with the cardboard centred on top, and basting and pencil lines matching. Begin by folding over the fabric at each corner and securing it with masking tape.

2 Working first on one side and then the other, fold over the fabric on all sides and secure it firmly with pieces of masking tape, placed about 2.5cm (1in) apart. Also neaten the mitred corners with masking tape, pulling the fabric tightly to give a firm, smooth finish.

EXTENDING EMBROIDERY FABRIC

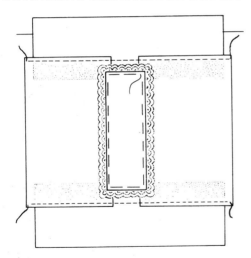

It is easy to extend a piece of embroidery fabric, such as a bookmark, to stretch it in a hoop.
● Fabric oddments of a similar weight can be used. Simply cut four pieces to size (in other words, to the measurement that will fit both the embroidery fabric and your hoop) and baste them to each side of the embroidery fabric before stretching it in the hoop in the usual way.

MOUNTING EMBROIDERY
The cardboard should be cut to the size of the finished embroidery, with an extra 6mm ($\frac{1}{4}$in) added all round to allow for the recess in the frame.

HEAVIER FABRICS

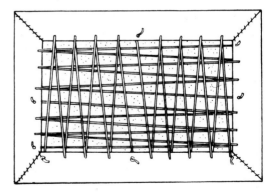

● Lay the embroidery face down, with the cardboard centred on top; fold over the edges of the fabric on opposite sides, making mitred folds at the corners, and lace across, using strong thread. Repeat on the other two sides. Finally, pull up the fabric firmly over the cardboard. Overstitch the mitred corners.

CROSS STITCH
For all cross stitch embroidery, the following two methods of working are used. In each case, neat rows of vertical stitches are produced on the back of the fabric.

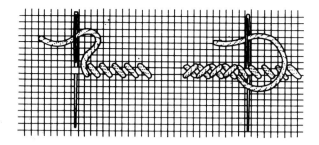

● When stitching large areas, work in horizontal rows. Working from right to left, complete the first row of evenly spaced diagonal stitches over the number of threads specified in the project instructions. Then, working from left to right, repeat the process. Continue in this way, making sure each stitch crosses in the same direction.

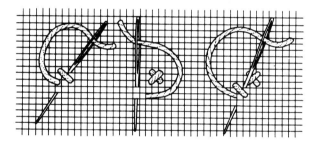

● When stitching diagonal lines, work downwards, completing each stitch before moving to the next. When starting a project always begin to embroider at the centre of the design and work outwards to ensure that the design will be placed centrally on the fabric.

BACKSTITCH

Backstitch is used in the projects to give emphasis to a particular foldline, an outline or a shadow. The stitches are worked over the same number of threads as the cross stitch, forming continuous straight or diagonal lines.

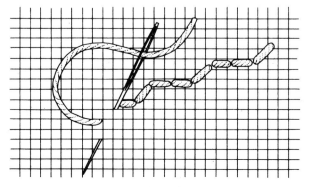

● Make the first stitch from left to right; pass the needle behind the fabric and bring it out one stitch length ahead to the left. Repeat and continue in this way along the line.

QUARTER CROSS STITCHES

Some fractional stitches are used on certain projects in this book; although they strike fear into the hearts of less experienced stitchers they are not difficult to master, and give a more natural line in certain instances. Should you find it difficult to pierce the centre of the Aida block, simply use a sharp needle to make a small hole in the centre first.

To work a quarter cross, bring the needle up at point A and down through the centre of the square at B. Later, the diagonal back stitch finishes the stitch. A chart square with two different symbols separated by a diagonal line requires two quarter stitches. Backstitch will later finish the square.

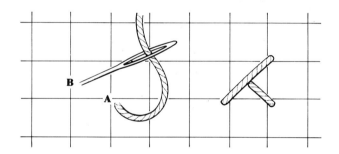

WORKING WITH WASTE CANVAS

Waste canvas has been used for two of the designs in 'The New Arrival'. This canvas, quite simply, provides a removable grid over which you can stitch on unevenly-woven fabrics. Once the design has been stitched, the canvas is removed. Firstly, determine the size of the design, and cut a piece of canvas that allows a border of at least 5cm (2in) all around. Baste the waste canvas to the design area of the fabric/item you are using. Stitch your design in the usual way, making sure it is centred on the fabric/item. When stitching is complete, remove the basting stitches and lightly dampen the canvas with water. Slowly and gently pull out the threads of canvas, *one at a time*, using a pair of tweezers. Don't hurry this process, as it could result in spoiling your stitching. You may need to re-dampen stubborn threads that will not pull out.

A Touch of
the Country

The borders and motifs featured here
would make a delightful addition to
any country-style room. With their
fresh colours and simple outlines,
these designs – shown here in sampler
form – could be used in a number of
ways, such as borders for linens and
towels, or as individual motifs to make
tiny pictures or other decorative items.

A TOUCH OF THE COUNTRY

YOU WILL NEED

For the Sampler, set in a frame measuring
23cm × 27cm (9in × 10½in):

*32.5cm × 37cm, (13in × 14½in) of 14-count
Fiddler's Lite Aida
Stranded embroidery cotton in the colours given
in the panel
No26 tapestry needle
Wooden frame of your choice
Strong cardboard, cut to fit into the
frame recess
Strong thread, for lacing across the back
when mounting*

•

THE EMBROIDERY

Prepare the fabric, marking the centre with horizontal and vertical lines of basting stitches, and set it in a frame (see page 5). Count out from the centre to start cross stitching at a convenient point. Work the embroidery, completing all the cross stitching first, using two strands of embroidery cotton in the needle, and making sure that all the top crosses lie in the same direction. Finish with the backstitching, made with one strand in the needle.

When stitching is complete, handwash the piece if necessary and press gently on the wrong side. Leave the basting stitches in position at this stage; they will provide useful guidelines when mounting, see below.

MOUNTING THE SAMPLER

Mark the central horizontal and vertical lines on the cardboard and align these with the lines of basting stitches. Lace the embroidery over the mount, following the instructions on page 6, and remove basting stitches.

Set the mounted picture in your chosen frame. A simple wooden frame, with no mount, has been used here, but you might prefer to surround the sampler with a cardboard mount, selecting one of the pastel shades used in the embroidery. Seal the back of the frame with broad tape, to protect the sampler from dust.

TOP

A TOUCH OF THE COUNTRY ▲		DMC	ANCHOR	MADEIRA
•	White	White	2	White
S	Clear green	3363	262	1311
●	Dark grey brown	640	903	1905
P	Medium dusky pink	224	893	0813
I	Light dusky pink	225	892	0501
L	Medium grey green	522	860	1513
▲	Dark muted grey	3022	392	1905
V	Very light grey brown	644	830	1907

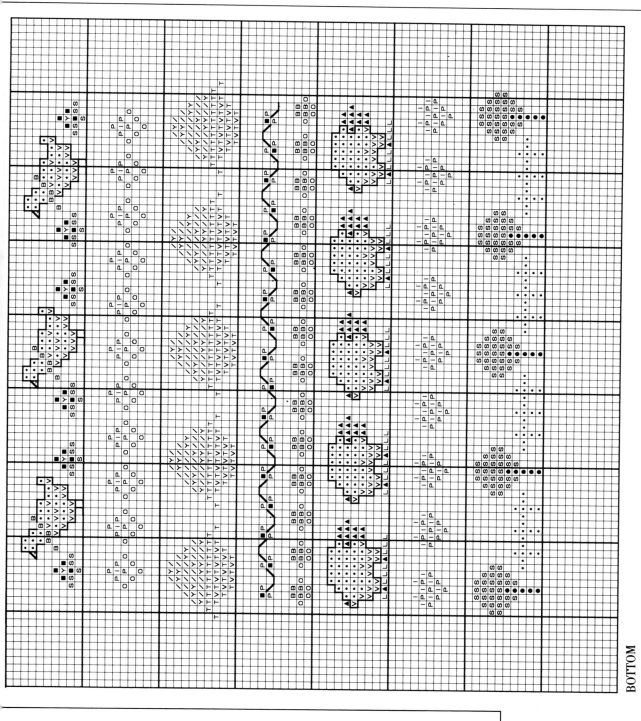

BOTTOM

		DMC	ANCHOR	MADEIRA
O	Medium yellow green	3053	844	1510
B	Light antique blue	932	920	1710
■	Dark dusky pink	223	895	0812
Y	Medium gold	676	891	2208
T	Medium grey brown	642	853	1906
/	Very light grey green	524	858	1511
N	Light golden brown	613	831	2109
	Medium muted grey*	3023	1040	1903

Note: use medium muted grey* (used for bks only) to backstitch sheep and geese outlines; clear green for the pink flower border, and white for the window panes.

Victorian Florals

Floral motifs are a perennial favourite with stitchers, lending themselves to a multitude of uses and occasions. These delicately shaded Victorian rose and lilac designs have been finished in several ways, but you can use them as you please, filling your home with the beauty of stitched blooms.

VICTORIAN FLORALS

YOU WILL NEED

For the silver pendant, measuring approximately 4cm × 4.8cm (1½in × 1⅞in):

*13cm (5in) square of 22-count, antique white Hardanger fabric
Stranded embroidery cotton in the colours given in the panel
No26 tapestry needle
Pendant, for suppliers see page 48*

For the frosted glass bowl, with a circular top 6.8cm (2⅝in) in diameter:

*13cm (5in) square of 18-count, antique white Aida fabric
Stranded embroidery cotton in the colours given in the panel
No26 tapestry needle
Frosted glass bowl, for suppliers see page 48*

For the porcelain box, with an oval lid measuring 7cm × 5cm (2⅞in × 2in)

*3cm (5in) square of 18-count, antique white Aida fabric
Stranded embroidery cotton in the colours given in the panel
No26 tapestry needle
Porcelain box, for suppliers see page 48*

For the picture, in a circular frame measuring 6.5cm (2½in) in diameter:

*13cm (5in) square of 18-count, antique white Aida fabric
Stranded embroidery cotton in the colours given in the panel
No 26 tapestry needle
Circular frame, for suppliers see page 48*

●

THE EMBROIDERY

If you are stitching all the motifs that are on Aida fabric, or several copies of one motif, you may be able to economize by using just one piece of fabric, but make sure that you leave an adequate amount of space for your purposes around each design.

For each design, use one strand of cotton in the needle. Make sure that all the top crosses run in the same direction.

When you have finished, gently steam press the embroidery on the wrong side. Set the embroidery in the chosen object, following the manufacturer's assembly instructions.

THE COUNTRY ▶		DMC	ANCHOR	MADEIRA
	Medium mauve*	3041	871	0806
◣	Very light grey green	524	858	1511
S	Medium grey green	522	860	1513
T	Light mauve	3042	870	0807
−	Very light mauve	3743	869	0801
●	Dark salmon pink	3712	10	0416
O	Medium salmon pink	760	9	0405
X	Light salmon pink	761	8	0404
·	Very light salmon pink	3713	48	0502

Note: use medium mauve (used for backstitch only) to outline the bow.*

PICTURE ▶		DMC	ANCHOR	MADEIRA
◣	Very light grey green	524	858	1511
S	Medium grey green	522	860	1513
●	Dark salmon pink	3712	10	0416
X	Light salmon pink	761	8	0404
·	Very light salmon pink	3713	48	0502

PENDANT AND PORCELAIN BOWL ▶		DMC	ANCHOR	MADEIRA
Y	Medium yellow	744	301	0112
◣	Very light grey green	524	858	1511
S	Medium grey green	522	860	1513
T	Light mauve	3042	870	0801
−	Very light mauve	3743	869	0806
●	Dark salmon pink	3712	10	0416
O	Medium salmon pink	760	9	0405
X	Light salmon pink	761	8	0404
·	Very light salmon pink	3713	48	0502

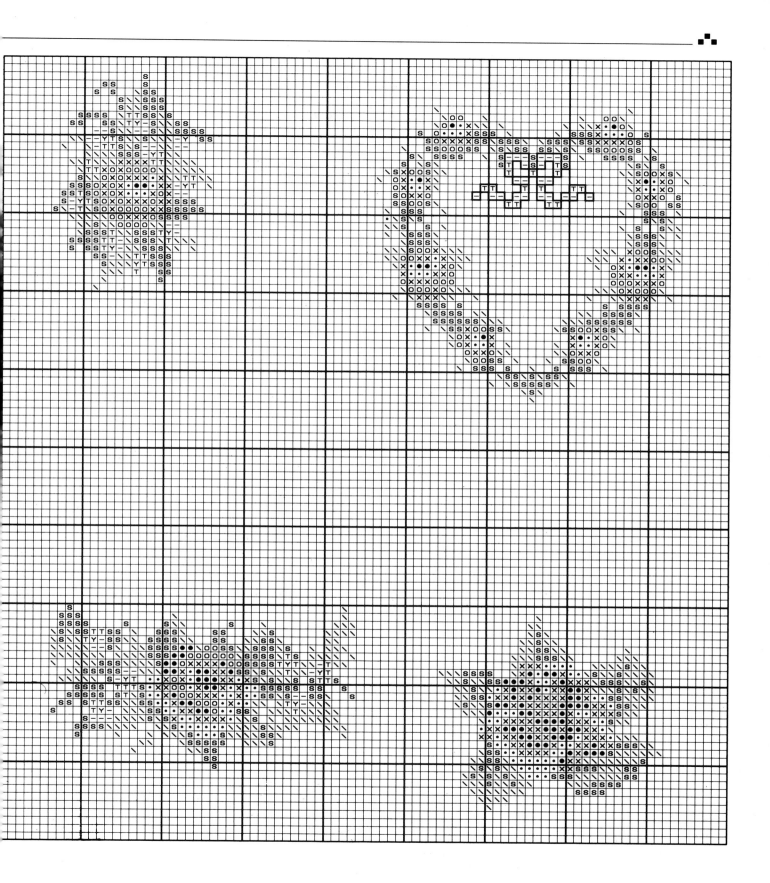

The New Arrival

The arrival of a new addition to the family is always a cause for great joy — and the decoration of nursery items and clothing is a lovely and lasting way of celebrating this special occasion. Here are several baby motifs used in different ways; they could also be applied to baby linens, used as tiny nursery pictures or to decorate other items of clothing and the like.

THE NEW ARRIVAL

For the Teddy Bear card, with an oval aperture measuring 6.5cm × 8cm (2½in × 3¼in):

10cm × 15cm (4in × 6in) of white, 18-count Aida fabric
Ribbon trim (optional)
Stranded embroidery cotton in the colours given in the appropriate panel
No26 tapestry needle
Purchased card, for suppliers see page 48

For the baby vest and socks:

Approximately 20cm × 15cm (8in × 6in) of waste canvas
Stranded embroidery cotton in the colours given in the appropriate panel
No24 tapestry needle
Purchased vest and socks, or other items of clothing

For the baby bib:

Stranded embroidery cotton in the colours given in the appropriate panel
No24 tapestry needle
Purchased bib, for suppliers see page 48

•

THE EMBROIDERY

For the card, prepare the fabric (see page 4) and either set it in a hoop or stitch with it in the hand. Use one strand of thread in the needle throughout, for cross stitches and backstitching.

Trim the finished embroidery to measure slightly larger all round than the card window, then centre it behind the window, using the basting stitches as guidelines. Make light pencil marks on the back of the embroidery and the back of the window, to act as registration marks. Remove the basting stitches, then replace the card in the window. Use double-sided tape to secure the card in position, then press the backing down firmly. Attach the ribbon trim, if desired, with either a dab of fabric glue or a piece of double-sided tape.

For the vest and socks, prepare the items by basting waste canvas pieces in position over the design areas and stitch over the canvas (see page 7).

Use two strands of embroidery cotton in the needle for cross stitches and one for backstitching. When you have finished, remove the waste canvas threads.

For the baby bib, also use two strands for cross stitches and one for backstitching.

TEDDY BEAR ▶		DMC	ANCHOR	MADEIRA
B	Pale blue	3752	343	1710
O	Pale shell pink	3713	48	0502
S	Pale yellow	745	300	0111
·	White	White	2	White
■	Dark golden brown	610	889	2119
X	Light tan	738	361	2013
V	Very light tan	739	366	2014
T	Golden tan	437	362	2012

Note: use dark golden brown for all backstitching.

ROCKING HORSE ▶		DMC	ANCHOR	MADEIRA
B	Pale blue	3752	343	1710
O	Pale shell pink	3713	48	0502
P	Medium salmon pink	761	8	0404
■	Dark golden brown*	610	889	2119
Y	Medium yellow	744	301	0112

Note: use dark golden brown (not used for cross stitching) for all backstitching and to make a french knot for the eye.*

CHICK ▶		DMC	ANCHOR	MADEIRA
B	Pale blue	3752	343	1710
S	Pale yellow	745	300	0111
■	Dark golden brown*	610	889	2119
Y	Medium yellow	744	301	0112

Note: use dark golden brown (not used for cross stitching) for all backstitching and to make a french knot for the eye.*

PRAM ▶		DMC	ANCHOR	MADEIRA
B	Pale blue	3752	343	1710
O	Pale shell pink	3713	48	0502
P	Medium salmon pink	761	8	0404
■	Dark golden brown	610	889	2119
X	Light tan	738	361	2013
V	Very light tan	739	361	2014
T	Golden tan	437	362	2012

Note: use dark golden brown for all backstitching

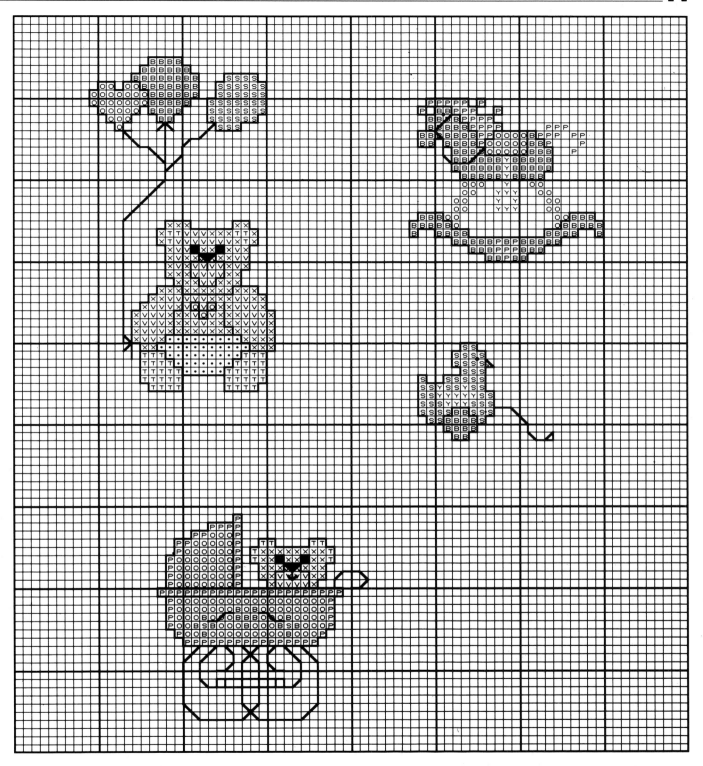

Special Occasion Borders

Scattered through the year are a number of festivals, such as Christmas or Easter, and celebrations, including birthdays or Mother's Day. This selection of borders has been designed with these special occasions in mind. The borders can be used for many different items, from table linen to bookmarks, or you might choose to use individual motifs for placecards, or for small gifts or mementoes.

SPECIAL OCCASION BORDERS

YOU WILL NEED

14-count Aida Ribband, 5cm (2in) wide, in your chosen colour
Stranded embroidery cotton in the colours given
No24 tapestry needle
Graph paper and coloured pencils or felt-tip pens (optional)

NOTE: Aida Ribband is available in a number of colours and widths. The length that you require will depend on the end use of the embroidered band. The panel lists all the colours used in the complete range of borders, so check which shades are used in your chosen border and buy one skein each of those particular colours only.

•

PLANNING THE DESIGN

Start by establishing the desired length of your border, so that you can then calculate the required number of repeats for that length. Unless the design is very long, the easiest way to do this is to use graph paper, as shown in the charts in this book. Remember that each graph square represents one Aida block, so with 14-count Aida, 14 squares will represent 2.5cm (1in). Start with a motif at the centre of the band and work outwards in each direction, adjusting the space between motifs as necessary to finish with a complete repeat at each end, and making sure that you leave additional space – at least 6mm (¼in) – for turning the ends under if, for example, the band is to be stitched to a towel.

If you wish to fill a length exactly, you may be able to adjust the space between repeats by inserting extra stitches into the linking sections.

ASSEMBLY

Start by finding the centre of the band and marking it with vertical and horizontal lines of basting stitches. Stitch the central motif/repeat, making sure that you leave an even space above and below, and work out to the sides. Two strands of cotton were used in the needle for cross stitching, and one for backstitching.

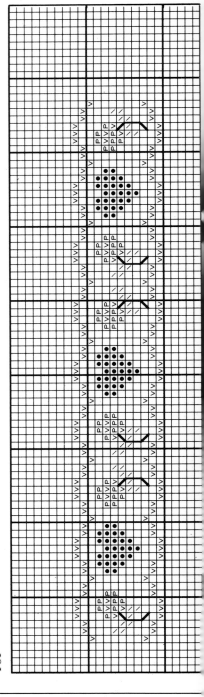

TOP

SPECIAL OCCASION BORDERS ▶		DMC	ANCHOR	MADEIRA
⊡	White	White	02	White
●	Dark salmon pink	760	09	0405
P	Medium salmon pink	761	08	0404
V	Pale shell pink	3713	48	0502
◿	Very pale grey green	524	858	1511
S	Light yellow	745	300	0111
△	Medium yellow	744	301	0112
▲	Dark golden brown	610	889	2119
R	Light golden brown	612	832	2108

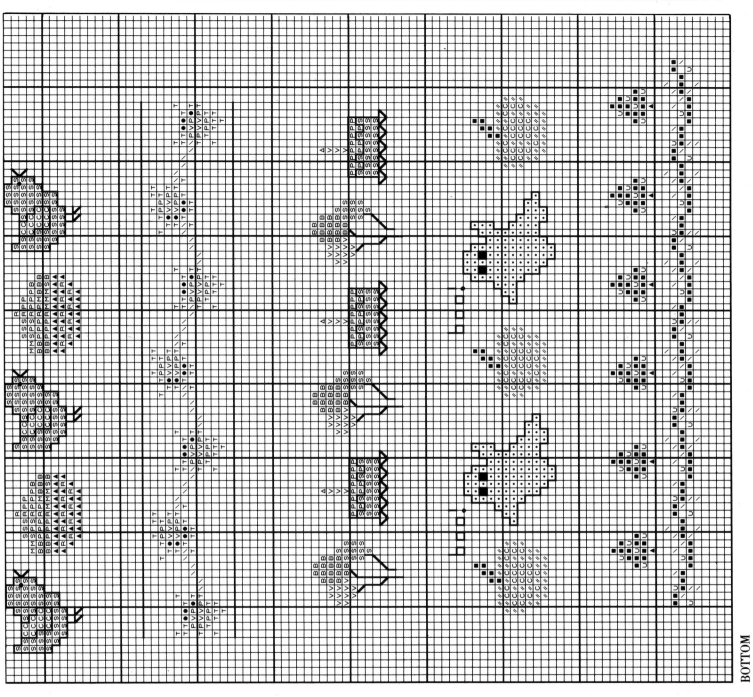

		DMC	ANCHOR	MADEIRA
T	Medium grey green	522	860	1513
B	Pale blue	3752	343	1710
M	Medium lilac	554	0711	96
■	Clear green	3363	262	1602
⁄	Medium soft orange	3776	1048	0310
C	Light orange	402	1047	2307
U	Light red	3328	1024	0406
	Dark grey*	414	233	1801

Note: backstitch the stems of Border 1 in medium grey green; the chickens of Border 2 in dark golden brown; the lines at the top and bottom of Border 3 in very pale grey green; the balloon strings, cake and lace of Border 4 and the ghost outline and lettering of Border 5 in dark grey* (used for backstitching only).

Floral Alphabet

Floral monograms make very special stitched gifts; two border designs are given with the alphabet, one featuring peach diamonds and small flowers, and the other with peach rosebuds and hearts. Who could fail to appreciate an initialled gift with these delicate floral touches?

FLORAL ALPHABET

YOU WILL NEED

For the framed initial, in a wooden frame measuring 15cm (6in) square:

25cm (10in) square of 14-count, antique white Aida fabric
Stranded embroidery cotton in the colours given in the panel
No26 tapestry needle
Frame of your choice

For the gift card, with an aperture measuring 6.5cm (2½in) square:

13cm (5in) square of 22-count, cream Hardanger fabric
Stranded embroidery cotton in the colours given in the panel
No26 tapestry needle
25cm (10in) of peach ribbon, 4mm (⅙in) wide, if desired
Gift card, for suppliers see page 48

For the lacy pillow, measuring 14cm (5½in) square, including the lace edging:

15cm (6in) square of 18-count, white damask Aida fabric
12cm (4¾in) square of white cotton or damask, to back the pillow
50cm (20in) of pre-gathered lace edging, 2cm (¾in) deep
Peach ribbon bow
Stranded embroidery cotton in the colours given in the panel
No26 tapestry needle
Loose polyester filling

•

CENTRING AN INITIAL

Prepare the fabric for your chosen design, marking the centre with horizontal and vertical lines of basting (see page 4). It is important to make sure that your chosen initial is centred on the fabric. To find the centre of an initial, count the number of squares across at the widest point of the initial, and count the number of squares down at the longest point. Divide each measurement by two, and count up and inwards to find the centre.

Count out from the centre of the fabric and start stitching at a convenient point.

FRAMED INITIAL

Complete the embroidery, using two strands of embroidery thread in the needle for the cross stitch and one for backstitching. Surround the initial with the Peach and Rosebud border. Press the finished embroidery on the wrong side, using a steam iron. Lace it over a cardboard mount (see page 6) and set it in your chosen frame.

GIFT CARD

Complete the embroidery, surrounding your chosen initial with the Peach Diamond border. Use one strand of cotton in the needle throughout and take each stitch over one thread of linen. Lightly press the embroidery on the wrong side with a steam iron. Trim it to fit neatly behind the aperture of the card, and complete the card, following the manufacturer's instructions. Finish with a ribbon tie, if desired.

LACY PILLOW

Complete the embroidery, surrounding your chosen initial with the Peach and Rosebud border. Use one strand of cotton in the needle throughout. Handwash the finished embroidery and lightly press on the wrong side with a steam iron.

Trim the fabric to measure 12cm (4¾in) square. Pin the lace around the embroidery, with the decorative edge facing inwards and the straight edge just within the 1cm (¾in) seam allowance. Join lace ends and, with right sides together, pin and stitch the backing fabric and lace-edged embroidery together, leaving a 5cm (2in) gap at one side. Clip across the seam allowance at the corners; turn the cover right side out; fill with polyester, and slipstitch the opening. Stitch a ribbon bow to one corner.

FLORAL ALPHABET AND BORDERS ▶	DMC	ANCHOR	MADEIRA
B Medium blue grey	927	849	1708
Light blue grey*	928	900	1709
Medium grey green*	522	860	1513
S Light grey green	524	858	1511
• Light peach	950	881	2309
X Medium dusky peach	3773	882	2310
● Dark dusky peach	407	883	2312

Note: light blue grey* is used for the Peach and Rosebud border only; medium grey green* is used for the Peach Diamond border only; for the Peach and Rosebud border, backstitch the lacy edge in light blue grey and the hearts in dark dusky peach.

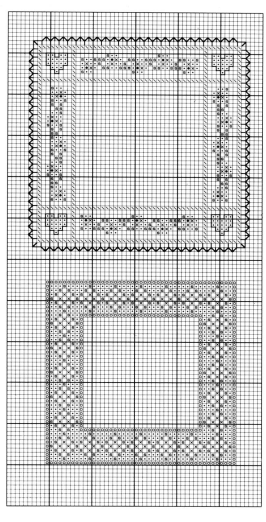

BORDERS

ALPHABET

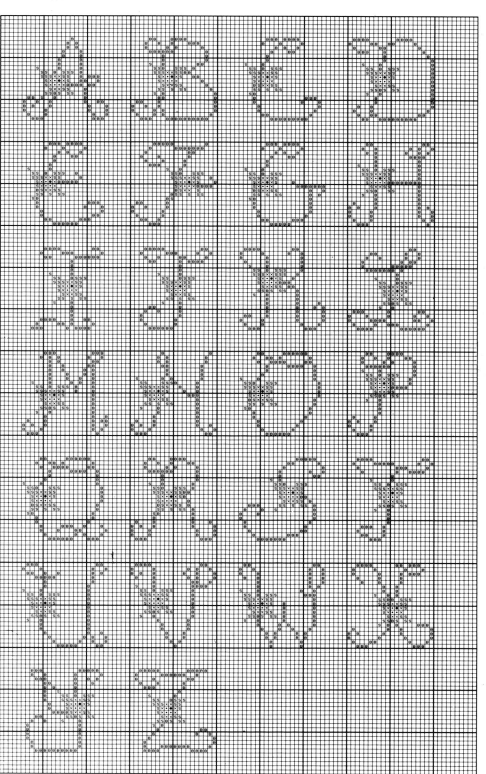

A Special Day

Bluebirds, hearts, roses and ribbons in soft shades of peach and delicate blue – these are the perfect accessories for a wedding. These motifs have been used in various ways to create a range of pretty and lasting gifts and mementoes for the bridal couple or other members of the wedding group.

A SPECIAL DAY

YOU WILL NEED

For the coaster, measuring 5.5cm (2¼in) in diameter:

12.5cm (5in) square of antique white, 18-count Aida fabric
Stranded embroidery cotton in the colours given in the appropriate panel
No26 tapestry needle
Glass coaster, for suppliers see page 48

For the card, with a rectangular aperture measuring 13cm × 7cm (5¼in × 3¾in):

12.5cm × 18cm (5in × 7½in) of antique white, 18-count Aida fabric
Peach-coloured ribbon trim, 7mm (⅓in) wide, if desired
Stranded embroidery cotton in the colours given in the appropriate panel
No26 tapestry needle
Card, for suppliers see page 48

For the picture, set in an oval frame measuring 7cm × 5.5cm (2⅞in × 2¼in):

15cm × 20cm (6in × 8in) of antique white, 18-count Aida fabric
Stranded embroidery cotton in the colours given in the appropriate panel
No26 tapestry needle
Silver frame, for suppliers see page 48

For the placecard:

Small remnant piece of antique white, 18-count Aida fabric
Stranded embroidery cotton in the given colours given in the appropriate panel
No26 tapestry needle
Placecard, for suppliers see page 48

For the gift card:

Small remnant piece of antique white, 18-count Aida linen
Peach ribbon, 3mm (⅛in) wide, for a trim
Stranded embroidery cotton in the colours

in the appropriate panel
No26 tapestry needle
Gift card, for suppliers see page 48

NOTE: You will also require some graph paper and a pencil, to work out the names and dates. The panel lists all the colours used in the complete range of projects, so check which colours are used in your chosen project(s) and buy one skein each of those particular colours only.

•

PLANNING THE DESIGN

Several alphabets and numerals have been provided with these designs, so that you can personalize the items by adding names for initials and dates. Work these out on graph paper (each square represents one Aida block). Ensure that names and dates are centred under the other parts of the design, to give a pleasing effect. If the names are very long, you may need either to use a smaller alphabet or to stitch the initials only.

Each design uses only a small amount of fabric, which makes these projects an ideal way of using up off-cuts. On the other hand, if you have no odd pieces of fabric, you may prefer to embroider designs in batches, to avoid waste.

For each design, prepare the fabric as described on page 4, and mark the horizontal and vertical centre lines with basting stitches in a light-coloured thread. Set the fabric in a hoop and count out from the centre to start stitching at a point convenient to you. Each design is stitched with one strand of thread throughout, to give a delicate effect.

Work all cross stitches first, making sure that all top stitches run in the same direction. Finally, work all backstitch details.

Gently handwash the finished piece, if necessary, and lightly press with a steam iron on the wrong side. Follow the manufacturer's instructions for assembly.

A SPECIAL DAY ▶	DMC	ANCHOR	MADEIRA
• White	White	2	White
X Pale peach	754	1012	0305
P Medium peach	3779	868	0403
● Dark peach	758	9575	0402
S Medium grey green	522	860	1513

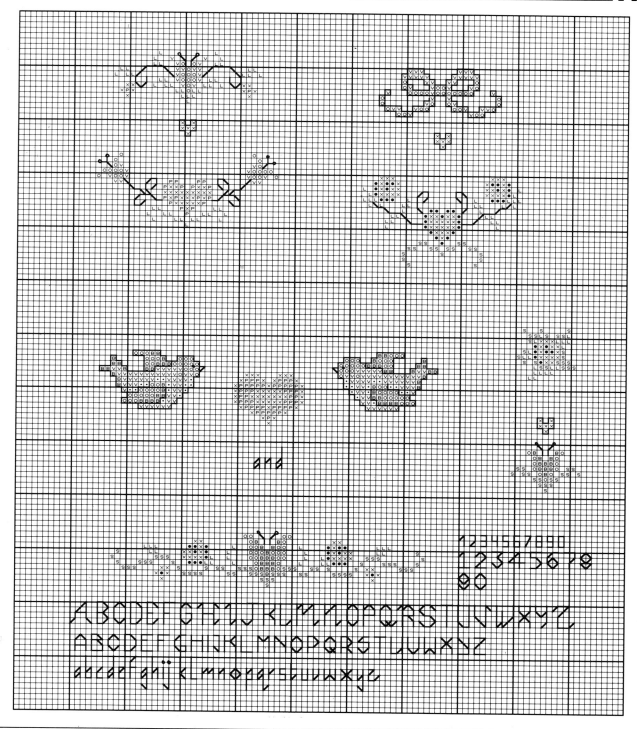

		DMC	ANCHOR	MADEIRA
L	Very light grey green	524	858	1511
V	Very light grey blue	928	900	1709
O	Light grey blue	927	849	1708
B	Medium grey blue	926	850	1707
	Medium steel grey*	646	815	1811

Note: for the coaster, backstitch the stems in medium grey green; the heart in dark peach, and lettering and stamens in medium steel grey*. For the card, make french knots for the eyes and backstitch the birds' outlines and beaks, and the lettering in medium steel grey*. For the oval picture, backstitch the bow outline in medium grey blue; the stems in medium grey green, and the heart in dark peach. For the gift card, backstitch the initials and heart in dark peach and the stamens in medium steel grey* . Medium steel grey* is used for backstitch only.

A Victorian Christmas

The Victorian era provides the theme for these richly-coloured ornaments. Inserted into small frames, they would prove ideal for hanging on a tree, but the same motifs could be used for greeting cards, gift tags, or the placecards on your Christmas dinner table.

A VICTORIAN CHRISTMAS

YOU WILL NEED

For each motif, set in a frame measuring
6.5cm (2½in) in diameter:

*Approximately 10cm (4in) square of ivory,
18-count Adia fabric
Stranded embroidery cotton in the colours given
in the appropriate panel
Balger blending filament in gold, one spool
No26 tapestry needle
Approximately 20cm (8in) of ribbon,
6mm (¼in) wide, optional, for a bow
Round gold-coloured frame, for suppliers
see page 48*

*NOTE: if you are stitching all the motifs, you will
only need one skein of each colour.*

•

THE EMBROIDERY

Each design uses only a small amount of fabric, and
to avoid any waste you may prefer to embroider
designs in batches. For each motif, prepare the
fabric as described on page 4, and mark the
horizontal and vertical centre lines with basting
stitches in a light-coloured thread. Set the fabric in
a hoop and count out from the centre to start
stitching at a point convenient to you. Work all cross
stitches first, making sure that all top stitches run in
the same direction. Finally, work all backstitch
details.

Use one strand of embroidery cotton in the needle
when making cross stitches and half-stitches, and
also for backstitching. Gently handwash the finished
piece, if necessary, and lightly press with a steam
iron on the wrong side.

ASSEMBLY

Use the clear plastic from the frame to trim the
embroidery to a size that will fit in the frame. Centre
the design in the frame, and carefully push in the
snap-in back. Trim with a ribbon bow, if desired.

VICTORIAN BOW ▶		DMC	ANCHOR	MADEIRA
P	Dark salmon	760	9	0405
O	Light pink red	3328	11	0406
	Dark red*	347	19	0407
X	Apple green	320	216	1311
L	Light green	368	240	1310
	Very dark brown*	839	891	2208
▲	Medium gold	676	891	2208 }

used together with one strand of Balger blending filament in gold ⎬

Note: use very dark brown to outline the bow, and dark red* for the
background lines (both shades are used for bks only).*

CHRISTMAS BORDER ▶		DMC	ANCHOR	MADEIRA
P	Dark salmon	760	9	0405
	Light pink red*	3328	11	0406
●	Dark red	347	19	0407
X	Apple green	320	216	1311
S	Dark green	319	246	1405
▲	Very dark brown	839	380	1913
L	Medium gold	676	891	2208 }

used together with one strand of Balger blending filament in gold ⎬

Note: use light pink red (used for bks only) to outline the hearts,
and one strand of medium gold with one strand of gold blending*

CHRISTMAS WELCOME ▶		DMC	ANCHOR	MADEIRA
O	Light pink red	3328	11	0406
●	Dark red	347	19	0407
X	Apple green	320	216	1311
S	Dark green	319	246	1405
B	Medium beige brown	841	378	1911
＼	Light beige brown	842	378	1910
·	White	White	1	White
	Very dark brown*	839	380	1913
C	Medium gold	676	891	2208 }

used together with one strand of Balger blending filament in gold ⎬

Note: use very dark brown (used for bks only) to outline the door.*

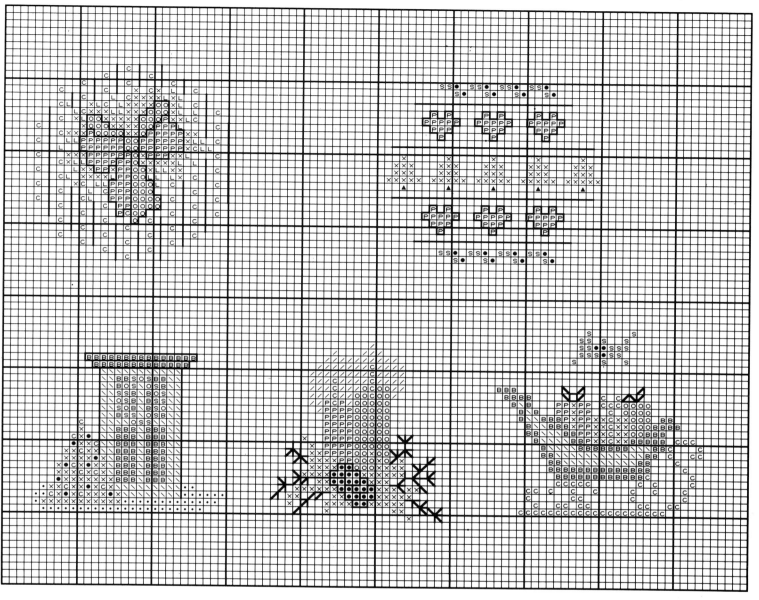

CHRISTMAS LIGHTS ▲	DMC	ANCHOR	MADEIRA
P Dark salmon	760	9	0405
O Light pink red	3328	11	0406
● Dark red	347	19	0407
X Apple green	320	216	1311
Dark green*	319	246	1405
⁄ Light gold			
(half cross stitch only)	677	886	2205
Very dark brown*	839	380	1913
C Medium gold	676	891	2208 ⎫

used together with one strand of Balger blending filament in gold ⎭

Note: outline the holly berries in very dark brown* and backstitch the fir branches in dark green* (both used for bks only).

SLEIGH ▲	DMC	ANCHOR	MADEIRA
P Dark salmon	760	9	0405
O Light pink red	3328	11	0406
● Dark red	347	19	0407
X Apple green	320	216	1311
Dark green*	319	246	1405
B Medium beige brown	841	378	1911
\ Light beige brown	842	376	1910
C Medium gold	676	891	2208 ⎫

used together with one strand of Balger blending filament in gold ⎭

Traditional Borders

Old samplers often feature a number of borders, usually formed from flowers, fruit or geometric shapes. The borders in this section have been stitched together in the form of a 'strip sampler', which was a traditional way of reminding the stitcher of various patterns. Of course, each border can be used by itself in a variety of ways – on table linens, clothing, linen bands and so on.

TRADITIONAL BORDERS

YOU WILL NEED

*33cm × 38cm (11in × 13in) of linen-look, 25-count
Jobelan fabric
Stranded embroidery cottons in the colours given
in the panel
No24 tapestry needle
Strong thread for lacing across the back when
mounting
Stiff cardboard for mounting
23cm × 28cm (9in × 11in) wooden frame of
your choice*

•

THE EMBROIDERY

Prepare the fabric, basting across the centre with
horizontal and vertical lines, and stretch it in a
frame (see page 5). Following the chart, start the
embroidery at the centre of the design, using two
strands of thread in the needle and making each
cross stitch over two fabric threads. Finish by
backstitching around the eyes, using one strand of
thread in the needle.

Leaving the basting stitches in position, gently
steam press the finished embroidery on the wrong
side.

MOUNTING

You can use either of the methods described on page
7 to mount your embroidery. To achieve a smooth
finish, you may find that it is helpful to secure the
fabric to the edge of the board with pins, working
from the centre point out to both corners, and then
repeat for the opposite side, to make sure that the
fabric is even and taut. Secure with tape or lacing,
and then repeat for the remaining sides. Remove
basting stitches.

If you are setting the mounted fabric in the frame
yourself, use rustproof pins to secure the backing
board, and seal the back of the picture with broad
tape, to ensure that dust cannot enter the frame.

USING THE BORDERS

Individual borders can easily be taken and used on
Aida ribband to decorate table and other linens, see
pages 28-31.

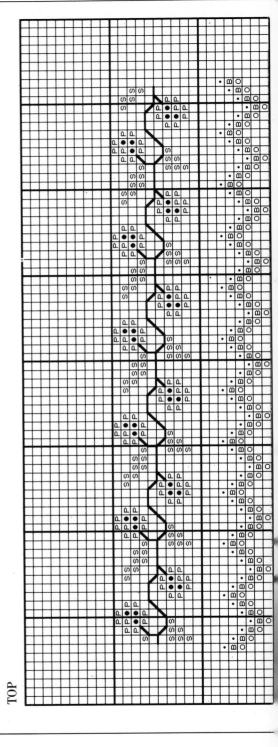

TOP

TRADITIONAL BORDERS ▶		DMC	ANCHOR	MADEIRA
P	Medium dusky peach	950	881	2309
●	Dark dusky pink	3773	882	2310
S	Very light grey green	524	858	1511
V	Medium grey green	522	860	1813
O	Dark blue grey	926	850	1707
B	Medium blue grey	927	849	1708

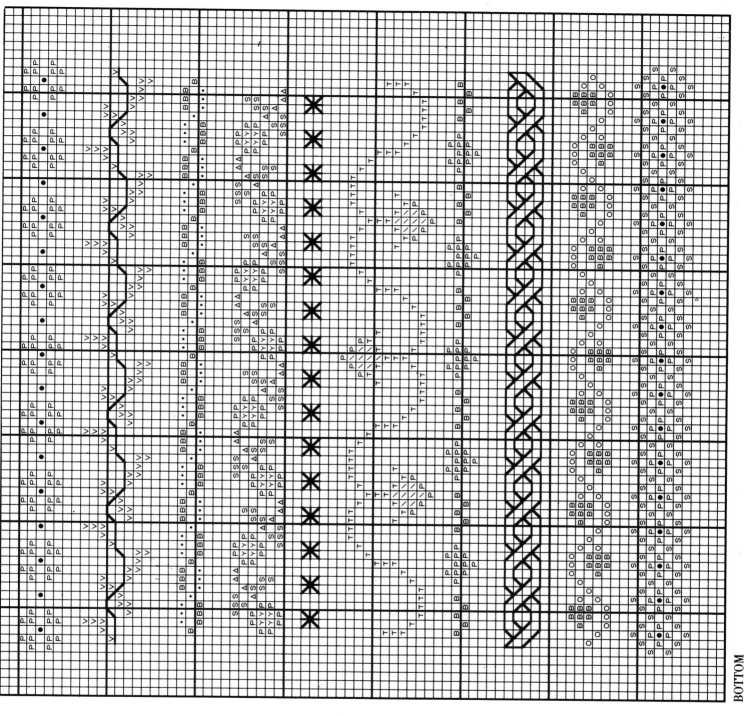

	DMC	ANCHOR	MADEIRA
· Light blue grey	928	900	1709
◣ Pale dusky peach	3774	778	1910
T Medium grey brown	642	853	1906
Y Medium gold	676	891	2208
B Medium yellow green	3053	844	1510

Note: backstitch the stems in row 1 in medium grey green and those in row 4 in medium grey brown; for row 7, which is in backstitch only, use dark dusky peach, or a colour of your choosing, and similarly, for row 10, use medium grey green.

Finishing Touches

The tradition of decorating fine home
linens with embroidery is currently
enjoying a revival of interest, with a
number of linens being created
specifically with the stitcher in mind.
These delicately-shaded floral borders
and motifs have been stitched on
purchased hand towels with Aida
inserts, but they could be used in a
number of ways on other items of
your choice.

FINISHING TOUCHES

YOU WILL NEED

For each handtowel:

*Stranded embroidery cotton in the colours given
in the appropriate panel
No26 tapestry needle
Hand towel, for suppliers see page 48*

*NOTE: if you are stitching all the designs, to make a
set of four towels, you will only require one skein
of each colour*

●

THE EMBROIDERY

The important consideration is to ensure that you balance the repeats evenly across the towel, and leave an even amount of linen above and below the embroidery. Find the centre of the linen band by folding the towel, and baste down the centre. Also baste across the centre of the linen band, from side to side of the towel.

Centring the design on the linen band, begin stitching, working outwards to each side. Use two strands of embroidery cotton in the needle for cross stitching and one for backstitching details. Ensure that all the top crosses lie in the same direction. When you have finished, remove the basting stitches.

ROSE MOTIF ▶		DMC	ANCHOR	MADEIRA
S	Very light grey green	524	858	1511
O	Light shell pink	3713	48	0502
P	Medium salmon pink	761	8	0404
•	Very pale pink	819	271	0501
M	Pale antique mauve	3042	870	0806
Y	Medium yellow	744	301	0112
	Medium grey green*	522	860	1513

Note: backstitch stems in medium grey green (used for bks only).*

ROSE CREEPER ▶		DMC	ANCHOR	MADEIRA
S	Very light grey green	524	858	1511
O	Light shell pink	3713	48	0502
P	Medium salmon pink	761	8	0404
	Medium grey green*	522	859	1513

Note: backstitch decorative lines in very light grey green and stems in medium grey green (used for bks only).*

LACE AND BOUQUETS ▶		DMC	ANCHOR	MADEIRA
S	Very light grey green	524	858	1511
O	Light shell pink	3713	48	0502
P	Medium salmon pink	761	8	0404
•	Very pale pink	819	271	0501
X	Medium grey green	522	860	1513
L	Pale silver grey	762	397	1804
M	Pale antique mauve	3042	870	0806
	Dark antique mauve*	3041	870	0806

Note: backstitch the bows in dark antique mauve (used for bks only).*

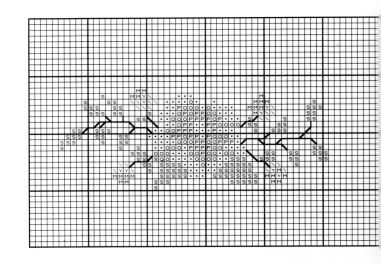

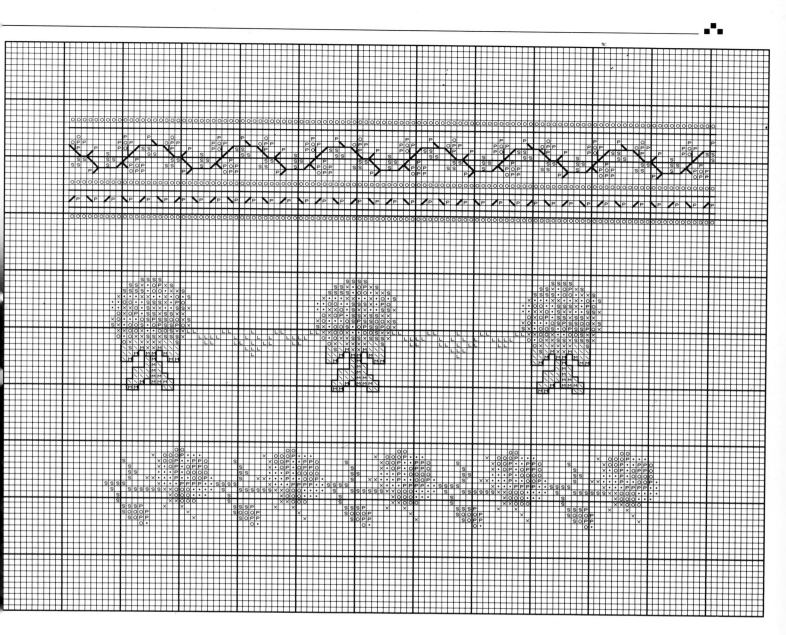

SUMMER ROSES ▲		DMC	ANCHOR	MADEIRA
S	Very light grey green	524	858	1511
O	Light shell pink	3713	48	0502
P	Medium salmon pink	761	8	0404
•	Very pale pink	819	271	0501
X	Medium grey green	522	860	1513

Antique Bears

Teddy bears never seem to lose their popularity – either in their own right, or as motifs for embroiderers – and justifiably so. This charming trio is stitched in muted shades to give them that well-loved, faded look common to bears; they would make delightful gifts, or you might just stitch them for yourself!

ANTIQUE BEARS

YOU WILL NEED

For each bear:

*10cm (4in) square of antique white, 18-count
Aida fabric
Stranded embroidery cotton in the colours given
in the appropriate panel
No26 tapestry needle*

For the patchwork bear:

*A frosted glass bowl, 6.5cm (2¹/₂in) in diameter, for
suppliers see page 48*

For the garden bear:

*An oval porcelain box, in ivory,
7cm × 5cm (2⁷/₈in × 2in), for suppliers see page 48*

For the heart bear:

*A cream card, 8.5cm × 6.5in (3³/₈in × 2¹/₂in), for
suppliers see page 48*

•

THE EMBROIDERY

For each bear, prepare the fabric, marking the centre each way with a horizontal and vertical line of basting stitches (see page 4). If you are embroidering all three designs, you may find it easier to use one large piece of fabric, dividing the separate areas with basting stitches and then marking the centre of each, as described.

One strand of thread is used throughout for all designs. Work all the cross stitches first, making sure that top stitches all lie in the same direction, and then add the backstitch details.

When you have finished the embroidery, wash the fabric, if necessary, and press it lightly on the wrong side. Leave the basting stitches in position at this stage.

THE EMBROIDERY

For the glass bowl and the oval box, follow the manufacturer's instructions. In each case, use the template provided to mark the shape on the fabric, with the basting stitches still in position to help you to ensure that the design is centred. Trim

and remove basting stitches, then insert the embroidery into the lid as directed.

For the card, trim the embroidery to measure about 12mm (¹/₂in) larger than the opening, each way, using the basting stitches as a guide to ensure that the design is centred. Remove basting stitches; place the embroidery behind the opening, and seal the card.

PATCHWORK BEAR ▶		DMC	ANCHOR	MADEIRA
■	Very dark brown	3031	905	2003
●	Medium tan	435	369	2010
T	Light tan	347	943	1910
I	Pale golden tan	738	361	2013
•	Very pale golden tan	739	366	2014
P	Medium salmon pink	761	8	0404
U	Light shell pink	3713	48	0502
M	Medium lilac	544	97	0711
B	Medium antique blue	932	920	1710

Note: backstitch body and features in very dark brown.

GARDEN BEAR ▶		DMC	ANCHOR	MADEIRA
	Very dark brown*	3031	905	2003
P	Medium salmon pink	761	8	0404
U	Light shell pink	3713	48	0502
B	Medium antique blue	932	920	1710
▲	Dark golden brown	610	889	2119
X	Light golden brown	612	832	2108
O	Very light golden brown	613	831	2109
–	Pale cream	712	926	2101
⁄	Very pale grey green	524	858	1511
N	Medium grey green	522	860	1513
C	Medium blue	3752	343	1710

Note: backstitch body and features in very dark brown (used for bks only), and the stems of the flowers in medium grey green.*

HEART BEAR ▶		DMC	ANCHOR	MADEIRA
	Very dark brown*	3031	905	2003
P	Medium salmon pink	761	8	0404
U	Light shell pink	3713	48	0502
B	Medium antique blue	932	920	1710
◣	Pale silver grey	762	397	1804
◢	Dark beige brown	839	380	1913
R	Medium beige brown	840	354	1912
S	Light beige brown	841	378	1911
V	Very light beige brown	842	376	1910

Note: backstitch body and features in very dark brown (used for bks only).*

ACKNOWLEDGMENTS

Once again I would like to thank Terry for his love and encouragement; thanks must also go to the various friends and fellow stitchers who have given me valuable input and encouragement during my designing career. A word of thanks, too, to Heather, my editor, and all at Merehurst who have been involved in this book; to Mike Grey at Framecraft Miniatures for supplying products for many of my designs, and the staff of Outlines Picture Framers, 22 the Pavement, Clapham, London, for their friendly and efficient service in framing 'A Touch of the Country' and 'Traditional Borders'.

SUPPLIERS

The following mail order company has supplied some of the basic items needed for making up the projects in this book:

Framecraft Miniatures Limited
372/376 Summer Lane
Hockley
Birmingham, B19 3QA
England
Telephone (021) 359 4442

Addresses for Framecraft stockists worldwide
Ireland Needlecraft Pty Ltd
2-4 Keppel Drive
Hallam, Victorian 3803
Australia

Danish Art Needlework
PO Box 442, Lethbridge
Alberta T1J 3Z1
Canada

Sanyei Imports
PO Box 5, Hashima Shi
Gifu 501-62
Japan

The Embroidery Shop
286 Queen Street
Masterton
New Zealand

Anne Brinkley Designs Inc.
246 Walnut Street
Newton
Mass. 02160
USA

S A Threads and Cottons Ltd.
43 Somerset Road
Cape Town
South Africa

For information on your nearest stockist of embroidery cotton, contact the following:

DMC

UK
DMC Creative World Limited
62 Pullman Road
Wigston
Leicester, LE8 2DY
Telephone: 0533 811040

USA
The DMC Corporation
Port Kearney Bld.
10 South Kearney
N.J. 07032-0650
Telephone: 201 589 0606

AUSTRALIA
DMC Needlecraft Pty
P.O. Box 317
Earlswood 2206
NSW 2204
Telephone: 02599 3088

COATS AND ANCHOR

UK
Kilncraigs Mill
Alloa
Clackmannanshire
Scotland, FK10 1EG
Telephone: 0259 723431

USA
Coats & Clark
P.O. Box 27067
Dept CO1
Greenville
SC 29616
Telephone: 803 234 0103

AUSTRALIA
Coats Patons Crafts
Thistle Street
Launceston
Tasmania 7250
Telephone: 00344 4222

MADEIRA

UK
Madeira Threads (UK) Limited
Thirsk Industrial Park
York Road, Thirsk
N. Yorkshire, YO7 3BX
Telephone: 0845 524880

USA
Madeira Marketing Limited
600 East 9th Street
Michigan City
IN 46360
Telephone: 219 873 1000

AUSTRALIA
Penguin Threads Pty Limited
25-27 Izett Street
Prahran
Victoria 3181
Telephone: 03529 4400

Aida Ribband and the baby bib used in 'The New Arrival' can be obtained from:
Wimble Bees, Unit 4, Manor Farm Barns, Wantage, OXON OX12 8NE. Telephone: (0235) 771731.